Saving Grandma's Special Day the Country Way
(A Book of Rhymes and Consonant Blends)

Habakkuk Educational Materials

Published by Habakkuk Educational Materials

Copyright © 2019-2022 Habakkuk Educational Materials. All rights reserved.

SAVING GRANDMA'S SPECIAL DAY THE COUNTRY WAY
(A Book of Rhymes and Consonant Blends)

Copyright © 2019-2022 by Habakkuk Educational Materials

No part of this book without a reproducible notice affixed to the footnote may be reproduced in any form or by any electronic or mechanical means, including information storage and retrieval systems, without the written consent of the publisher. If a page is specified as reproducible, the reproduction is permitted for non-commercial, classroom use only. Please address your inquiries to Habakkuk@cox.net.

ISBN (Paperback Edition): 978-1-954796-19-5

Image on the front cover: © wizdata1/Shutterstock.com

Interior illustrations: Copyrighted images are used under license from stock.adobe.com and Shutterstock.com.

Printed and bound in the United States of America

Published by Habakkuk Educational Materials

Visit www.habakkuk.net

Content included in this book:

1. Consonant blends chart
2. Short story full of consonant blends
3. Discussion questions about the short story
4. Consonant blends worksheets

Saving Grandma's Special Day the Country Way is packed full of rhymes and consonant blends. The book begins with a chart that illustrates 26 consonant blends (also known as consonant clusters) that are used in the English language. There are consonant blends that begin with *s*, blends that end with *r*, and blends that end with *l*. There is also a *tw* blend. In a consonant blend such as *st* in *stop*, the consonant *s* still makes the /s/ sound and *t* still makes the /t/ sound, but they slide together so smoothly that it seems like you're only hearing one sound.

The 26 blends from the chart can be found within the sentences of the story, and tasks listed at the bottom of the pages ask students to find and circle specific blends on the page when they begin a word. Following the story, there is a list of discussion questions that can be answered by girls and boys over what was read. The questions are followed by a number of reproducible worksheets that teach children what a consonant blend is and provides them ample practice in sounding out words with these sounds.

The story itself rhymes and is about some grandchildren who want to honor their grandmother by buying her a gift. They run into a problem when their uncle's truck will not start, and they have no way to get to town. The older children, however, quickly come up with a witty solution, and thus Grandma's special day is saved the country way!

To contact Habakkuk Educational Materials, please visit the website below.

https://www.habakkuk.net/

Free consonant blends coloring sheets (see the examples below) are also available by visiting the "Free Teaching Materials" page of the Habakkuk Educational Materials website.

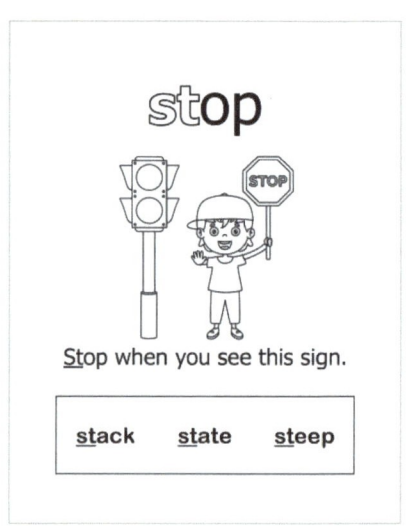

Instructions: Name the letters, identify the sound, and read the illustrated word; eBook readers can click the arrow to hear the sounds. The pauses in the recording are to give students time to repeat what is said.

Consonant Blends	bl black	cl clean
fl fly	gl gloves	pl place
sl sleep	br bright	cr crayon
dr draw	fr fruit	gr green
pr pretty	tr try	tw twins
sc scorpion	sk sky	sm small
sn snow	sp spider	st stop
sw swing	scr scroll	spl splash
spr spread	str strange	squ square

Today we are planning a surprise for Grandma,
although her birthday is still a month away,
just to show our love and gratitude
for what she does for us every day.

Grandma Carole is at a prayer meeting
and will not be back till this afternoon,
and we have things to do,
so we better get started soon.

Task: Seven words on this page begin with a consonant blend. Find and circle the consonant blends **pl**, **pr**, **gr** (there are three of them), and **st** (there are two of them).

Uncle Bubba is glad to drive us into town
so that we can get everything we need.
We want to buy a special present,
and he needs some animal seed.

But then something happened
that nearly ruined it all.
"My blue truck will not start,"
I heard Uncle Bubba call.

Task: Seven words on this page begin with a consonant blend. Find and circle the consonant blends **bl**, **dr**, **gl**, **pr**, **sp**, **st**, and **tr**.

"Whenever I turn the switch,
it makes a squeaking noise.
We will have to skip the store today.
Please tell Mandi and the boys."

Mandi is my little sister,
and her twin brother is Mike.
I also have a brother named David,
and he and I love to hike.

Task: Eight words on this page begin with a consonant blend. Find and circle the consonant blends **br** (there are two of them), **pl**, **sk**, **squ**, **st**, **sw**, and **tw**.

The twins were not in the house
when I walked in the door.
I wonder where they could be!
They left their toys all over the floor!

I did tell David about the truck,
and you could tell that he was sad,
but then he glanced out the window
and blurted out an idea that he had.

Task: Five words on this page begin with a consonant blend. Find and circle the consonant blends **bl**, **fl**, **gl**, **tr**, and **tw**.

Indeed, he sprung to his feet and screamed, "Jimmy, I know just what to do!
We can drive the tractor!
There's room enough for two."

Task: Four words on this page begin with a consonant blend. Find and circle the consonant blends **dr**, **scr**, **spr**, and **tr**.

When we asked Uncle Bubba if it was alright,
he thought our plan was pretty smart,
and in a split second we scurried off to the
tractor that would get us to the country mart.

Although the tractor is slow,
we think we can get there before they close.
And, yes indeed, we made it,
and guess what gift we chose!

Task: Nine words on this page begin with a consonant blend. Find and circle the consonant blends **cl**, **pl**, **pr**, **sc**, **sl**, **sm**, **spl**, and **tr** (there are two of them).

If you really want to know,
I'll give you a strong hint--
every time girls put it on,
you smell a pretty scent!

Task: Three words on this page begin with a consonant blend. Find and circle the consonant blends **pr**, **sm**, and **str**.

Grandma was praying with the twins
when we snuck in her gift.
When she opened her eyes,
she cried, "It's perfume!"
and then, of course, she sniffed.

Task: Six words on this page begin with a consonant blend. Find and circle the consonant blends **cr**, **gr**, **pr**, **sn** (there are two of them), and **tw**.

Story Questions

1. Where were the twins when their brothers could not find them?

2. Why were Grandma Carole's grandchildren planning to ger her a surprise?

3. What happened that almost prevented the children from getting their grandma a gift?

4. What solution did the two older children come up with so that they could still get to the store and buy her a present?

5. What was Grandma Carole doing when the boys brought in her gift?

6. What present did the boys pick out for Grandma?

7. The last sentence says that Grandma sniffed. Do you think she was sniffing her present, sniffing because she was crying happy tears, or both?

Bl Consonant Blend

Directions: Instruct students to pronounce a word. Then change the word by inserting a *b* in the space provided. Call on someone to pronounce the new word with the *bl* blend. When students have finished sounding out the words, use one or more of the words in a sentence.

Blend: In a consonant blend such as *bl*, the consonant *b* still makes the /b/ sound and *l* still makes the /l/ sound, but they slide together so smoothly that it seems like you're only hearing one sound.

_lab	_led	_lock
_lack	_lend	_loom
_lame	_less	_lot
_lank	_light	_low
_last	_limp	_lower
_leach	_link	_lush
_leak	_lob	_luster

_____

Reproducible for non-commercial, classroom use only by Habakkuk Educational Materials

Cl Consonant Blend

Directions: Instruct students to pronounce a word. Then change the word by inserting a *c* in the space provided. Call on someone to pronounce the new word with the *cl* blend. When students have finished sounding out the words, use one or more of the words in a sentence.

Blend: In a consonant blend such as *cl*, the consonant *c* still makes the /k/ sound and *l* still makes the /l/ sound, but they slide together so smoothly that it seems like you're only hearing one sound.

_lack	_lean	_lock
_lamp	_leave	_log
_lap	_left	_lot
_lash	_lever	_loud
_latter	_lick	_luck
_law	_link	_lump
_lay	_lip	_lung

Reproducible for non-commercial, classroom use only by Habakkuk Educational Materials

Fl Consonant Blend

Directions: Instruct students to pronounce a word. Then change the word by inserting an *f* in the space provided. Call on someone to pronounce the new word with the *fl* blend. When students have finished sounding out the words, use one or more of the words in a sentence.

Blend: In a consonant blend such as *fl*, the consonant *f* still makes the /f/ sound and *l* still makes the /l/ sound, but they slide together so smoothly that it seems like you're only hearing one sound.

_lag	_law	_lock
_lair	_lay	_loss
_lake	_led	_low
_lame	_lick	_lung
_lap	_lies	_lush
_lash	_light	_lute
_latter	_lip	_lying

Reproducible for non-commercial, classroom use only by Habakkuk Educational Materials

Pl Consonant Blend

Directions: Instruct students to pronounce a word. Then change the word by inserting a *p* in the space provided. Call on someone to pronounce the new word with the *pl* blend. When students have finished sounding out the words, use one or more of the words in a sentence.

Blend: In a consonant blend such as *pl*, the consonant *p* still makes the /p/ sound and /l/ still makes the /l/ sound, but they slide together so smoothly that it seems like you're only hearing one sound.

_lace	_lead	_lot
_lain	_led	_luck
_lane	_ledge	_lug
_late	_liable	_lump
_latter	_lied	_lunge
_lay	_lies	_lush
_layer	_light	_lying

Reproducible for non-commercial, classroom use only by Habakkuk Educational Materials

Sl Consonant Blend

Directions: Instruct students to pronounce a word. Then change the word by inserting an *s* in the space provided. Call on someone to pronounce the new word with the *sl* blend. When students have finished sounding out the words, use one or more of the words in a sentence.

Blend: In a consonant blend such as *sl*, the consonant *s* still makes the /s/ sound and /l/ still makes the /l/ sound, but they slide together so smoothly that it seems like you're only hearing one sound.

_lab	_lid	_lot
_lack	_light	_low
_lap	_lime	_lug
_late	_lip	_lumber
_led	_lit	_lump
_ledge	_liver	_lung
_lick	_lope	_lush

Reproducible for non-commercial, classroom use only by Habakkuk Educational Materials

Gl and *Dr* Consonant Blends

Directions: Instruct students to pronounce a word. Then change the word by inserting a *g* in the space provided under the "gl" heading or a *d* in the space provided under the "dr" headings. Call on someone to pronounce the new word with the *gl* or *dr* blend. When students have finished sounding out the words, use one or more of the words in a sentence.

Blend: In a consonant blend such as *gl*, the consonant *g* still makes the /g/ sound and /l/ still makes the /l/ sound, but they slide together so smoothly that it seems like you're only hearing one sound.

gl	*dr*	*dr*
_lad	_raft	_read
_litter	_rag	_ream
_loss	_rain	_rift
_love	_rank	_rink
_low	_raw	_rip

_____

_____

Reproducible for non-commercial, classroom use only by Habakkuk Educational Materials

Br Consonant Blend

Directions: Instruct students to pronounce a word. Then change the word by inserting a *b* in the space provided. Call on someone to pronounce the new word with the *br* blend. When students have finished sounding out the words, use one or more of the words in a sentence.

Blend: In a consonant blend such as *br*, the consonant *b* still makes the /b/ sound and *r* still makes the /r/ sound, but they slide together so smoothly that it seems like you're only hearing one sound.

_race	_ranch	_rim
_racket	_rave	_ring
_rag	_reach	_rink
_raid	_reed	_risk
_rain	_ride	_room
_rake	_ridge	_runt
_ran	_right	_rush

Reproducible for non-commercial, classroom use only by Habakkuk Educational Materials

Cr Consonant Blend

Directions: Instruct students to pronounce a word. Then change the word by inserting a *c* in the space provided. Call on someone to pronounce the new word with the *cr* blend. When students have finished sounding out the words, use one or more of the words in a sentence.

Blend: In a consonant blend such as *cr*, the consonant *c* still makes the /k/ sound and *r* still makes the /r/ sound, but they slide together so smoothly that it seems like you're only hearing one sound.

_rack	_rave	_rime
_raft	_rayon	_ripple
_ram	_ream	_rock
_ramp	_reed	_row
_rank	_reek	_rumble
_rash	_rest	_rush
_rate	_rib	_rust

Reproducible for non-commercial, classroom use only by Habakkuk Educational Materials

Gr Consonant Blend

Directions: Instruct students to pronounce a word. Then change the word by inserting a *g* in the space provided. Call on someone to pronounce the new word with the *gr* blend. When students have finished sounding out the words, use one or more of the words in a sentence.

Blend: In a consonant blend such as *gr*, the consonant *g* still makes the /g/ sound and *r* still makes the /r/ sound, but they slide together so smoothly that it seems like you're only hearing one sound.

_race	_reek	_rip
_rain	_rid	_room
_ram	_riddle	_round
_rant	_rill	_row
_rate	_rim	_ruff
_ray	_rime	_rumble
_reed	_rind	_runt

Reproducible for non-commercial, classroom use only by Habakkuk Educational Materials

Pr Consonant Blend

Directions: Instruct students to pronounce a word. Then change the word by inserting a *p* in the space provided. Call on someone to pronounce the new word with the *pr* blend. When students have finished sounding out the words, use one or more of the words in a sentence.

Blend: In a consonant blend such as *pr*, the consonant *p* still makes the /p/ sound and *r* still makes the /r/ sound, but they slide together so smoothly that it seems like you're only hearing one sound.

_**r**aise   _**r**ide   _**r**esent

_**r**ank   _**r**im   _**r**eserve

_**r**ay   _**r**ime   _**r**eside

_**r**each   _**r**ivet   _**r**esident

_**r**ecede   _**r**obe   _**r**esume

_**r**efer   _**r**od   _**r**eview

_**r**epay   _**r**oof   _**r**ice

Reproducible for non-commercial, classroom use only by Habakkuk Educational Materials

Fr and *Tr* Consonant Blends

Directions: Instruct students to pronounce a word. Then change the word by inserting an *f* in the space provided under the "fr" heading or a *t* in the space provided under the "tr" headings. Call on someone to pronounce the new word with the *fr* or *tr* blend. When students have finished sounding out the words, use one or more of the words in a sentence.

Blend: In a consonant blend such as *fr*, the consonant *f* still makes the /f/ sound and *r* still makes the /r/ sound, but they slide together so smoothly that it seems like you're only hearing one sound.

fr	*tr*	*tr*
_rail	_race	_ray
_rank	_rack	_rim
_reed	_rail	_rip
_right	_rain	_roll
_risky	_rash	_rust

_____

_____

Reproducible for non-commercial, classroom use only by Habakkuk Educational Materials

Tw and *Sc* Consonant Blends

Directions: Instruct students to pronounce a word. Then change the word by inserting a *t* in the space provided under the "tw" heading or an *s* in the space provided under the "sc" headings. Call on someone to pronounce the new word with the *tw* or *sc* blend. When students have finished sounding out the words, use one or more of the words in a sentence.

Blend: In a consonant blend such as *tw*, the consonant *t* still makes the /t/ sound and *w* still makes the /w/ sound, but they slide together so smoothly that it seems like you're only hearing one sound.

tw	*sc*	*sc*
_weak	_can	_coop
_weed	_car	_cope
_wig	_care	_core
_win	_cat	_corn
_witch	_cold	_cuff

_____

_____

Reproducible for non-commercial, classroom use only by Habakkuk Educational Materials

Sk, Sm, and Sn Blends

Directions: Instruct students to pronounce a word. Then change the word by inserting an *s* in the space provided. Call on someone to pronounce the new word with the *sk*, *sm*, or *sn* blend. When students have finished sounding out the words, use one or more of the words in a sentence.

Blend: In a consonant blend such as *sk*, the consonant *s* still makes the /s/ sound and *k* still makes the /k/ sound, but they slide together so smoothly that it seems like you're only hearing one sound.

sk	*sm*	*sn*
_ketch	_mall	_nag
_kid	_mash	_nail
_kin	_mile	_nap
_kipper	_mock	_nicker
_kit	_mug	_nip

_____

_____

Reproducible for non-commercial, classroom use only by Habakkuk Educational Materials

Sp Consonant Blend

Directions: Instruct students to pronounce a word. Then change the word by inserting an *s* in the space provided. Call on someone to pronounce the new word with the *sp* blend. When students have finished sounding out the words, use one or more of the words in a sentence.

Blend: In a consonant blend such as *sp*, the consonant *s* still makes the /s/ sound and *p* still makes the /p/ sound, but they slide together so smoothly that it seems like you're only hearing one sound.

_**p**ace	_**p**ending	_**p**ool
_**p**an	_**p**ike	_**p**ore
_**p**are	_**p**ill	_**p**ort
_**p**ark	_**p**in	_**p**ot
_**p**atter	_**p**ine	_**p**out
_**p**eak	_**p**it	_**p**un
_**p**eck	_**p**oke	_**p**utter

Reproducible for non-commercial, classroom use only by Habakkuk Educational Materials

St Consonant Blend

Directions: Instruct students to pronounce a word. Then change the word by inserting an *s* in the space provided. Call on someone to pronounce the new word with the *st* blend. When students have finished sounding out the words, use one or more of the words in a sentence.

Blend: In a consonant blend such as *st*, the consonant *s* still makes the /s/ sound and *t* still makes the /t/ sound, but they slide together so smoothly that it seems like you're only hearing one sound.

_table	_tart	_tool
_tack	_teal	_top
_tag	_team	_tore
_tale	_tick	_tow
_talk	_till	_tub
_tall	_tilt	_tuck
_tar	_tone	_tumble

Reproducible for non-commercial, classroom use only by Habakkuk Educational Materials

Sw and *Scr* Blends

Directions: Instruct students to pronounce a word. Then change the word by inserting an *s* in the space provided under the "sw" headings or the letters *sc* in the space provided under the "scr" heading. Call on someone to pronounce the new word with the *sw* or *scr* blend. When students have finished sounding out the words, use one or more of the words in a sentence.

Blend: In a consonant blend such as *sw*, the consonant *s* still makes the /s/ sound and *w* still makes the /w/ sound, but they slide together so smoothly that it seems like you're only hearing one sound.

sw	*sw*	*scr*
_wallow	_wept	__ram
_warm	_wig	__ramble
_way	_wing	__ream
_weep	_wish	__roll
_well	_witch	__rub

Reproducible for non-commercial, classroom use only by Habakkuk Educational Materials

Spl, Spr, and *Squ* Blends

Directions: Instruct students to pronounce a word. Then change the word by inserting the letters *sp* in the space provided under the "spl" and "spr" headings or the letter *s* in the space provided under the "squ" heading. Call on someone to pronounce the new word with the *spl, spr,* or *squ* blend. When students have finished sounding out the words, use one or more of the words in a sentence.

Blend: In a consonant blend such as *spl*, the consonant *s* still makes the /s/ sound, *p* still makes the /p/ sound, and *l* still makes the /l/ sound, but they slide together so smoothly that it seems like you're only hearing one sound.

spl	*spr*	*squ*
__lash	__rain	_quad
__latter	__rang	_quash
__lice	__ray	_quid
__lint	__ring	_quire
__lit	__rung	_quirt

Reproducible for non-commercial, classroom use only by Habakkuk Educational Materials

Str Consonant Blend

Directions: Instruct students to pronounce a word. Then change the word by inserting the letters *st* or the letter *s* in the space provided to form words with the *str* blend. Call on someone to pronounce the new word with the blend. When students have finished sounding out the words, use one or more of the words in a sentence.

Blend: In a consonant blend such as *str*, the consonant *s* still makes the /s/ sound, *t* still makes the /t/ sound, and *r* still makes the /r/ sound, but they slide together so smoothly that it seems like you're only hearing one sound.

str

__rain
__ranger
__raw
__ray
__ream

__ride
__ring
__ripe
__roller
__rut

str

_**tr**ainer
_**tr**ap
_**tr**ip
_**tr**oll
_**tr**uck

Reproducible for non-commercial, classroom use only by Habakkuk Educational Materials